Collins

Primary Social Studies for Antigua and Barbuda

STUDENT'S BOOK
GRADE 2

Anthea S Thomas

Published by Collins
An imprint of HarperCollins*Publishers*
The News Building
1 London Bridge Street
London SE1 9GF

HarperCollins*Publishers*
Macken House, 39/40 Mayor Street Upper,
Dublin 1, D01 C9W8, Ireland

Browse the complete Collins Caribbean catalogue at
www.collins.co.uk/caribbeanschools

© HarperCollins*Publishers* Limited 2020
Maps © HarperCollins*Publishers* Limited 2020, unless otherwise stated

10 9 8 7 6 5

ISBN 978-0-00-840282-2

British Library Cataloguing-in-Publication Data
A catalogue record for this publication is available from the British Library.

Author: Anthea S. Thomas
Publisher: Elaine Higgleton
In-house senior editor: Julianna Dunn
Development & copy editor: Sue Chapple
Proof reader: Mitch Fitton
Cover designers: Kevin Robbins and Gordon MacGilp
Cover image: Wectors/Shutterstock
Typesetter: QBS
Illustrators: Danielle Boodoo-Fortuné
Production controller: Lyndsey Rogers

Printed and bound in the UK using 100%
Renewable Electricity at CPI Group (UK) Ltd

The publishers gratefully acknowledge the permission granted to reproduce the copyright material in this book. Every effort has been made to trace copyright holders and to obtain their permission for the use of copyright material. The publishers will gladly receive any information enabling them to rectify any error or omission at the first opportunity.

Printed and Bound in the UK using 100% Renewable Electricity at CPI Group (UK) Ltd

Acknowledgements

The publishers wish to thank the following for permission to reproduce photographs. Every effort has been made to trace copyright holders and to obtain their permission for the use of copyright materials. The publishers will gladly receive any information enabling them to rectify any error or omission at the first opportunity.
(t = top, c = centre, b = bottom, l = left, r = right)

p4: Shutterstock, p5: Shutterstock, p7: ART Collection/Alamy, p8tl: W. Scott McGill/SS, p8tr: Apaterson/SS, p8b: Joerg Steber/SS, p9: Everett Historical/SS, p13: Shutterstock, p14t: fizkes/SS, p14c: wavebreakmedia/SS, p14b: Shutterstock, p16t: wavebreakmedia/SS, p16bl: glenda/SS, p16br: Denise Andersen/SS, p17t: Anna Luopa/SS, p17c: Prostock-studio/SS, p17b: Rawpixel.com/SS, p18t: iofoto/SS, p18b: fizkes/SS, p19: Clive Chilvers/SS, p20t: ZoranKrstic/SS, p20c: art_of_sun/SS, p20b: Solomnikov/SS, p21t: sansak/SS, p21c: Willequet Manuel/SS, p21b: SusaZoom/SS, p22: Lorna Roberts/SS, p23: Afonkin_Y/SS, p26: Julinzy/SS, p27t: Atlaspix/SS, p27bl: Pixcellentprintsltd/SS, p27br: Isabelle Kuehn/SS, p28t: Don Mammoser/SS, p28b: Robert Fried / Alamy Stock Photo, p29: Shi Yali/SS, p30t: Paul B. Moore/SS, p30b: Barbara Arrindell, p31t: photowind/SS, p31b: Amy Katherine Dragoo / Alamy Stock Photo, p32: George Brice / Alamy Stock Photo, p33tl: Donianna Forde/SS, p33tr: Sarah Cheriton-Jones/SS, p33bl: EQRoy/SS, p33br: PlusONE/SS, p34tl: Barbara Arrindell, p34tr: Barbara Arrindell, p34b: The Museum of Antigua and Barbuda, p37t: byvalet/SS, p37bl: Cozine/SS, p37br: Anna Jedynak/SS, p38l: Africa Studio/SS, p38r: John T Takai/SS, p39tl: Cincila/SS, p39tr: Oleksandr_Delyk/SS, p39b: bergamont/SS, p40tl: Michael Hatfield / Alamy Stock Photo, p40tc: happiness time/SS, p40tr: FabrikaSimf/SS, p40b: ESB Professional/SS, p41tl: Okhumale Victor/SS, p41tr: Elize Lotter/SS, p41cl: Ratthaphong Ekariyasap/SS, p41cr: Alexander Raths/SS, p41bl: Abdol Majeed/SS, p41br: Lucia Pitter/SS, p42tl: sirtravelalot/SS, p42tr: Shutterstock, p42b: ittipon/SS, p43tl: Iakov Filimonov/SS, p43tr: from my point of view/SS, p43bl: UfaBizPhoto/SS, p43br: Africa Studio/SS, p44tl: Shutterstock, p44tr: Misunseo/SS, p44c: JEWEL SAMAD/AFP via Getty Images, p44b: Editor's own, p46: nuanz/SS, p47tl: Ivan C/SS, p47tr: William Perugini/SS, p47bl: Joseph Sohm/SS, p47br: Antho B/SS, p48tl: Melinda Nagy/SS, p48tr: Keeton Gale/SS, p48cl: Paolo Bona/SS, p48cr: Natursports/SS, p48bl: Radu Bercan/SS, p48bc: Vytautas Kielaitis/SS, p48br: dean bertoncelj/SS, p49t: Marc Boettcher / Alamy Stock Photo, p49b: BlueOrange Studio/SS, p50t: EQRoy/SS, p50b: Pincasso/SS, p51: EQRoy/SS, p52tl: Alena Nv/SS, p52tr: ds_vector/SS, p52c: Abscent/SS, p52bl: NAN728/SS, p52bc: Ramunas Bruzas/SS, p52br: quiggyt4/SS, p53tl: ATGImages/SS, p53tr: Mark Summerfield / Alamy Stock Photo, p53b: EQRoy/SS, p54tl: PJF Military Collection / Alamy Stock Photo, p54tr: Aviation Images Ltd / Alamy Stock Photo, p54bl: Andy Glenn/SS, p54br: Andmir/SS, p55: David Herraez Calzada/SS, p57t: beach rob / Alamy Stock Photo, p57b: Antigua and Barbuda Transport Board, p58: Antigua and Barbuda Transport Board, p60tl: SOMMAI/SS, p60tc: pukao/SS, p60tr: Olga Popova/SS, p60bl: akepong srichaichana/SS, p60br: Valentina Proskurina/SS, p61tl: Martin Charles Hatch/SS, p61tr: Findlay / Alamy Stock Photo, p62: GraphicsRF/SS, p63: Usagi-P/SS, p64t: Iakov Kalinin/SS, p64b: Drew McArthur/SS, p65t: al clark/SS, p65b: Paulo Miguel Costa/SS, p66t: John A Cameron/SS, p66c: Debbie Ann Powell/SS, p66b: juerginho/SS, p68: IgorZD/SS, p69t: fizkes/SS, p69b: wavebreakmedia/SS, p70t: PENDING, p70b: Ailsa Burn-Murdoch / Alamy Stock Photo, p71t: Editor's own, p71b: Quatrox Production/SS, p72: tanuha2001/SS.

Contents

1 Individuals in groups

We are learning to:

- understand the words 'individuals', 'group', 'community', 'ethnic group', 'nationality'
- name the first group of people who lived in Antigua and Barbuda
- describe how they lived
- list ethnic groups and nationalities living in Antigua and Barbuda today
- describe a settlement
- find parishes and villages on a map of Antigua and Barbuda
- name things people in a community have in common.

Being part of a group

This is Shania, who lives in Antigua. She is a single person. One person on their own is called an **individual**.

Individuals may belong to a **group**. A group is a set of people who have something in common. They may be a group of friends, they may work together, live together, or play a sport together.

Shania

A **family** is an example of a group. Families can be all different sizes.

This is Shania's family.

A group of people who live close together in a particular place make up a **neighbourhood**. Several neighbourhoods make up a **community**.

There are lots of different communities in Antigua and Barbuda. We can say that Antigua and Barbuda itself is one large community.

A typical community in Antigua and Barbuda

In a community there are houses that people live in. There are also churches and schools. You may find a supermarket, different shops, a police station and a post office. Often there is a playground for children, and some trees. Some communities are large, while others are small.

Communities of long ago

Long, long ago, before your parents and grandparents were born, other people lived in communities in Antigua and Barbuda. The first group of people that we know about were the Amerindians.

There were two groups of Amerindians: first the Arawaks and then later the Caribs. They came from South America to live in Antigua and Barbuda, and in other islands in the Caribbean. They came to the Caribbean in search of food.

The Carib name for Antigua was Waladli, and for Barbuda it was Wa'omoni.

Where did they live?

Like all people, the Amerindians needed water and food to survive. They settled near the sea and on land where the soil was good for growing crops. It was important to have fresh water to drink. Some of their communities in Antigua were in places that we now know as Jolly Beach, Indian Creek, Mamora Bay and Spanish Point.

ANCIENT CARIBS.

Here is a drawing of two Carib people.

They used canoes made from hollowed-out tree trunks to get from one place to the next. They got food from hunting and fishing and from the crops that they planted. The crops included cassava, sweet potato and yam.

The Amerindians used bones, volcanic stones, flintstones, shells and wood to make their tools.

The women learned how to make beautifu ornaments and pottery from the clay soil.

A place where people first come to live is called a **settlement**. Gradually, the settlements of the Amerindians became larger. The streams and rivers around them were used for transport and to water the crops.

The rivers were also used to get to other settlements in order to **trade**. This meant that they exchanged goods with other people. There was no money involved, so they didn't sell goods. Instead, it was called **bartering**.

Here you can see some typical huts they would have used for shelter, made from thatched leaves. This settlement would have been by a river so that they could easily transport their goods to trade with other settlers.

The Europeans

After the Amerindians came the Europeans. They planted crops such as sugar cane, and started rearing animals. The Europeans took the Amerindians to work on their plantations but many of them died quickly from the diseases that the Europeans brought to the island. They were also treated very badly.

The Europeans still needed people to work on their plantations, so then they took people from West Africa as **slaves**. The slaves had no freedom, they were forced to work very hard and were often beaten.

Slaves working on the sugar plantations.

Indians and Chinese

After slavery ended, the Europeans brought in Indians and Chinese to work for them. They did pay them but only very little. Some of these people later went back to India and China but others stayed on to start their own businesses.

Many different people

Soon, our island was filled with people who had come from many different countries.

We say that people who share a common background and way of life are an **ethnic group**. This means that they eat the same kind of food, do the same dance, dress in a similar way and believe the same things.

Today, many of the same ethnic groups who came here in the past make up the community of Antigua and Barbuda. They include Africans, Chinese, Indians and Syrians. The Indians and Chinese originally came as **indentured labourers** to work on the sugar plantations. The Syrians left their homes in the Middle East by their own free will, in order to escape persecution.

Nationalities

A country is also called a **nation**. When you are born in a country, you are called a national of that country and your **nationality** is named after that country. For example, people born in Antigua are called Antiguans, and those born in Barbados are Barbadians. As a national, you have all the rights that comes with belonging to that country.

There are many different nationalities and ethnic groups living in Antigua and Barbuda. These include:

- Africans
- Indians
- Chinese
- Barbadians
- Trinidadians
- Guyanese
- Jamaicans
- Hispanics
- Syrians
- Dominicans
- Americans

People in our community

The people who live in Antigua and Barbuda are all different:

- They have different religious beliefs. Some are Hindu, some are Muslim; others are Christian and Rastafarian.
- They are of different ages. Some are older, some are young adults, some are teenagers and some are children or babies.
- They have different jobs. Some are skilled workers, like carpenters, mechanics and electricians. Some are professional people, like teachers, doctors and lawyers. Other workers include police officers, firefighters, shopkeepers, maids and bankers.

There is one thing that is common to all people in our community, and that is that they should share and care for each other.

Antigua and Barbuda today

Antigua is divided into six parishes. These are:

- St. John
- St. Peter
- St. Paul
- St. Mary
- St. George
- St. Philip.

These parishes help us to identify the community that we live in.

Each parish has some villages, and some larger towns. You can see the parishes, and some of the towns and villages, on this map.

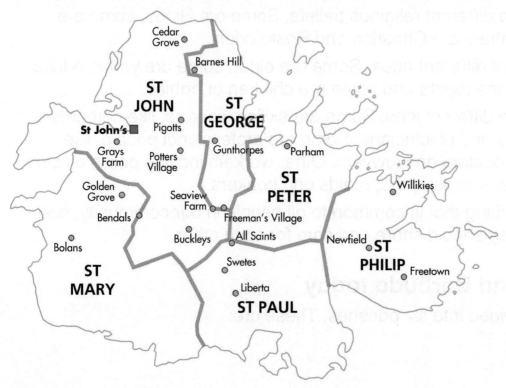

Antigua

Barbuda is considered to be one parish. Its main town is Codrington.

2 Living in Antigua and Barbuda

We are learning to:

- understand the words 'festival', 'dialect', 'folklore' and 'customs'
- name different types of family and their make-up
- describe how families change
- name some family and community celebrations
- list important ways to behave that are passed on in families
- understand how traditions are passed on
- compare how children lived long ago with how they live today.

What is a family?

A family is a group of people who are related to each other by blood or adoption. They usually live together.

This is Shania's family. She lives with her brother, mother and father.

Families are different

Some families have a mother and a father, with one or more children.

This is a **nuclear family**.

Some families only have a mother or a father, with a child or children. This is a **single-parent family**.

Some larger families have grandparents, aunts and maybe cousins living in the home, too. This is an **extended family**.

Family trees

We can use a family tree to show how people in our family are related to each other.

Members of a family love and care for each other.

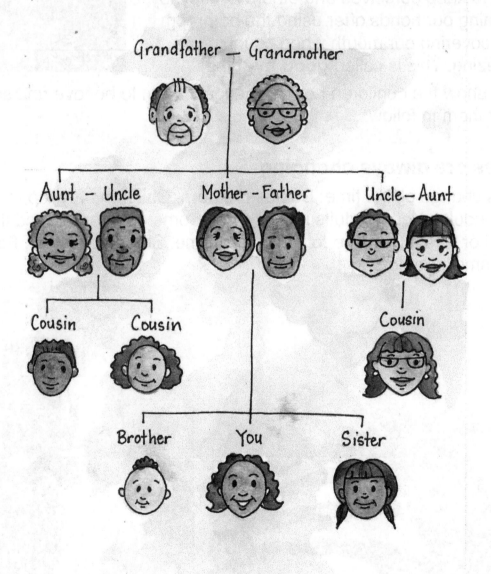

It is in our families that we first learn how to behave in our community. For example, we are taught:

- how to be kind and polite to others – saying please, thank you and excuse me.
- how to pray for each other.
- how to keep ourselves and others healthy, by washing our hands after using the bathroom and covering our mouth when coughing or sneezing. This is called **good hygiene**.

Parents show their children how they expect them to behave and set rules for them to follow.

Families are always changing

Families change all the time. Babies are born. Children grow up to become adults. Young adults leave home. Some get married and their husband or wife may come to live in the home. Some adults die. Families can get smaller or larger.

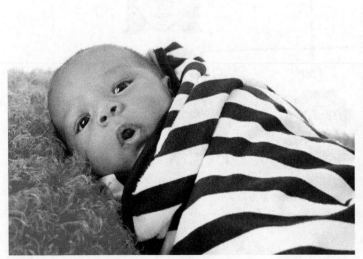

Changes like this can make members of the family happy or sad. They are happy when a baby is born or when a family member gets married but may be sad if they leave the home to start a family of their own. They are sad when a member of the family gets sick or dies.

Even though this is a sad occasion, when one member of the family dies, there is a funeral service to celebrate the person's life. The service is usually followed by eating and drinking.

Celebrations

Families often celebrate important events with each other. If someone has a birthday, there is usually a celebration with the whole family. Sometimes other people in the community are invited too.

Other family celebrations include:

The wedding of a family member. This is usually held in a church. It means two families are linked together, so people from both the bride's and the groom's family are there, as well as friends.

The date of the wedding is celebrated each year as the wedding anniversary. Couples do something special such as having dinner or going on a trip.

When a child does well at school, he or she may be given a reward or have a special dinner.

Community celebrations

This is when all the families come together to share in the fun. Some of these celebrations are festivals, which may carry on for two or more days.

Here are some important community celebrations:

Carnival

This festival is a celebration of our freedom from slavery. Carnival is held every summer in Antigua. Barbuda's festival is called Caribana and is celebrated during the Easter season.

Sailing Week

This festival of sailing is celebrated for one week each year, starting at the end of April. People from all over the world come to take part in the competition and to watch the fun.

Valentine's Day

This day of love is celebrated on the 14th of February each year. During this time, people show their love by giving cards and gifts to each other.

Easter

This is a Christian celebration to remember the death and resurrection of Jesus Christ. People go to church. On Easter Monday – the day that Jesus rose again – many people celebrate by going to the beach for a picnic.

Independence Day

Antigua celebrates its independence each year on the 1st of November. Lots of activities take place leading up to Independence Day. These include the National Food Fair where local foods that are a part of our culture are prepared and sold, School's Panorama and National Youth Rally.

Remembrance Day

This is on the 11th of November each year. It is a day to remember all the people who died in wars to serve their country.

Christmas

Christmas is the celebration of the birth of Jesus held on the 25th of December each year. Families get together and celebrate with food and drink, and by giving each other presents. Christmas is seen as a time of love and happiness.

Traditions

Families have all sorts of traditions, such as games they play, or a large family picnic or other meal. Parents and grandparents pass on these family traditions to children. It makes sure that traditions continue for a long time to come.

These sorts of traditions are part of our **culture**. Culture is the way of life of a group of people. The way people are accustomed to doing a thing is called its **customs**.

Traditions can be passed on by storytelling. At family gatherings, grandparents would tell young children stories of how things were done in the past.

Traditions are also passed on when craftsmen and women produce items that are a part of our culture, such as straw hats and straw bags.

During celebrations such as Independence Day, there is an emphasis on everything local so that young people learn about their cultural heritage.

Schools and churches are also places where our cultural traditions and heritage are learned.

Dialect is the language of our African ancestors and is considered our second language. It is easy to speak but hard to read and write. Dialect is very much a part of our culture.

Different cultures in the community

Each ethnic group in Antigua and Barbuda has its own culture and way of life.

Cultural differences can be seen by looking at the types of restaurants that are probably in your neighbourhood. For example, there may be Chinese restaurants that are famous for fried rice and chicken, Middle-Eastern restaurants famous for shawarma, and Jamaican restaurants that love to cook with jerk seasoning.

There are also various churches that people with different religious beliefs can attend.

As members of the Antiguan community, we need to be tolerant and show respect for these differences in culture.

Shawarma

How has life changed for children?

Long ago, life for children was very different from today. They didn't have the chance to go to school to learn to read and write. There was no television to watch. They didn't have the latest electronic gadgets to play with, like the games console you may have got for Christmas.

Instead, the girls helped their mothers with cooking, cleaning and planting crops, while the boys helped the men with hunting and fishing. They ate the food they caught and the fruit and vegetables they grew, because there were no fast-food restaurants. They did not take showers or sleep on a bed but instead bathed in rivers and slept on the floor of their mud houses.

Life was very different!

3 What does it mean to be Antiguan and Barbudan?

We are learning to:

- say why national symbols are important
- name the national symbols of Antigua and Barbuda
- list ways to show respect for national symbols
- name historical sites and buildings in Antigua and Barbuda
- describe how buildings have changed over time
- use a compass to give directions
- identify and use a scale and legend on a map.

National symbols

Countries in the Caribbean region share a similar culture. Each country has national symbols that help to identify that country and set it apart from the others.

Symbols are important because they show the history, culture and values we have as a country. This section is about the national symbols of Antigua and Barbuda.

- The national anthem was written by Sir Novelle Richards. It is sung during national ceremonies and celebrations, as well as in schools and churches.

Fair Antigua, We Salute Thee

Fair Antigua and Barbuda
We thy sons and daughters stand,
Strong and firm in peace or danger
To safeguard our native land.
We commit ourselves to building
A true nation brave and free.
Ever striving, ever seeking,
Dwell in love and unity.

Raise the standard! Raise it boldly!
Answer now to duty's call
To the service of thy country,
Sparing nothing, giving all;
Gird your loins and join the battle
'Gainst fear, hate and poverty,
Each endeavouring, all achieving,
Live in peace where man is free.

God of nations, let Thy blessings
Fall upon this land of ours;
Rain and sunshine ever sending,
Fill her fields with crops and flowers;
We her children do implore Thee,
Give us strength, faith, loyalty,
Never failing, all enduring
To defend her liberty.

- Antigua's motto – 'Each Endeavouring, All Achieving' – was written by Mr. James H Carrot. You can see it on the coat of arms on the opposite page. It is also a part of the national anthem.

- The national flag of Antigua and Barbuda was designed by Sir Reginald Samuel, in 1966. Each colour in the flag has a special meaning.

- ○ Gold – the start of a new era, like a rising sun
- ○ Red – the blood of slaves and the great energy of the people
- ○ Black – the soil and the African heritage
- ○ Blue – hope
- ○ The combination of yellow, blue and white represents the sun, sea and sand, while the 'V' shape represents victory.

- The coat of arms was originally designed by Mr. Gordon Christopher and was later changed a little by Mr. Don Cribbs. It shows various emblems of our culture.

  - The pineapple
  - Two fallow deer, one on either side of the shield
  - The shield
  - The sun, representing a new beginning
  - The colour black, representing our African heritage
  - The sugar mill, representing the importance of sugar in our past
  - The scroll, containing the national motto

- The national animal is the European fallow deer, found in Barbuda, and the national sea creature is the hawksbill turtle.

- The national bird is the frigate bird, which can be found in large numbers in Barbuda's Bird Sanctuary.

- The national flower is the dagger log flower.

- The national dish is pepperpot and fungi, which has been passed down from the Amerindians.
- The national fruit, the Antigua black pineapple, is known as the sweetest pineapple in the world.

- The national stone – petrified wood

- The national tree – the whitewood tree

- The **national weed** – the widdy widdy bush

- The **national dress** was designed by local artist Heather Doram, using traditional madras cotton material. It is usually worn during the Independence celebrations.

National heroes

National heroes are also symbols of a country. Only people who have done outstanding work for the country are given the title of national hero. In Antigua and Barbuda, the award is usually given during the Independence Day ceremony.

There are six national heroes of Antigua and Barbuda. Two of them are alive now. The photo shows four of our national heroes.

Prince Klass – he fought to free slaves.

Dame Nellie Robinson – she was a teacher who believed education must be for all children. She is the only woman to have been given the award of national hero.

Sir Vere Cornwall Bird (Snr) – he was the first Premier and Prime Minister of Antigua and Barbuda, after Independence. He fought for the rights of workers.

Sir George Walter was the second Premier of Antigua and Barbuda. He served the trade union and political movements for over 40 years.

Sir Isaac Vivian Alexander Richards (alive) – known as Viv Richards, he made Antigua and Barbuda known to the rest of the world, through cricket.

Sir Lester Bryant Bird – The other living hero was the former Prime Minister of Antigua and Barbuda. He also represented Antigua in athletics.

Showing respect to national symbols

As citizens of Antigua and Barbuda, we should show respect for our national symbols. Here are some ways to do it:

- Never throw the flag on the ground or damage it in any way.
- When the national anthem is being played, stand to attention – with your hands by your side, and looking straight in front of you.
- Be sure you know what the national symbols are!

Historical places and buildings

Antigua has a long history and there are many important historical places around the country. They are often visited by people who come to our islands. Here are just a few of them:

Betty's Hope, an old sugarcane plantation

Devil's Bridge in the northeast of the country

The Museum of Antigua and Barbuda, in St. John's

Nelson's Dockyard, in English Harbour, on the south coast

Modern buildings

Our landscape is always changing:

- Trees are cleared so that we can build houses and roads.
- Natural disasters like hurricanes can change the landscape.
- People learn new technologies and that changes the way houses are built.
- More people means less land space.

Compare these buildings. At the top you can see the National Library and the National Treasury in our capital, St. John's. Below, you can see the building that used to be home to those two organisations. What differences can you see?

The National Library, St John's.

The National Treasury, St John's.

The building which used to contain The National Library and The National Library in St. John's.

Using maps and giving directions

Points of a compass

We use North, South, East and West to give directions for getting from one place to another. For example, you might say that to get to school from your home, you have to go South.

You can give the location of various places in your community by using a compass. Most maps have a compass symbol. You can see the compass on the right on this map of Antigua, and on the left on this map of Barbuda.

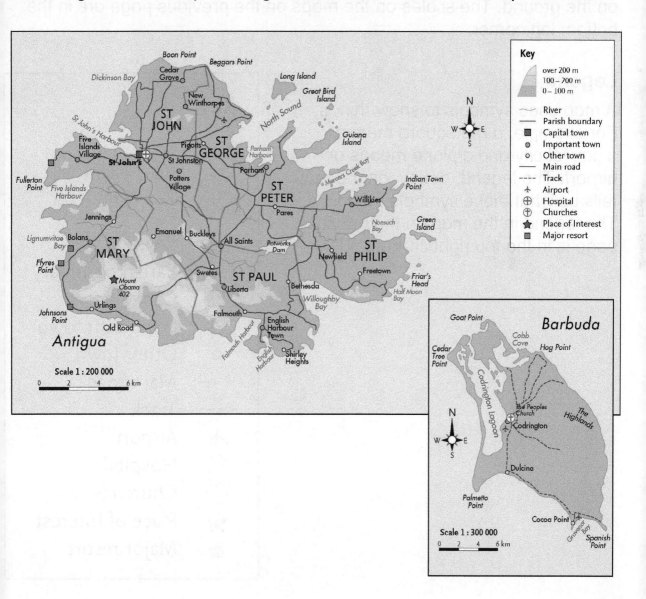

Scale

Scale 1 : 200 000

0   2   4   6 km

A scale is used to show how a distance on a map relates to the distance on the ground. The scales on the maps on the previous page are in the bottom left corner.

Legend

A map uses symbols to show things. For example, a red square means a capital city and a plane means an airport. The legend, or key, on the map tells us what these symbols mean. The legend in the map on the previous page is in the top right corner.

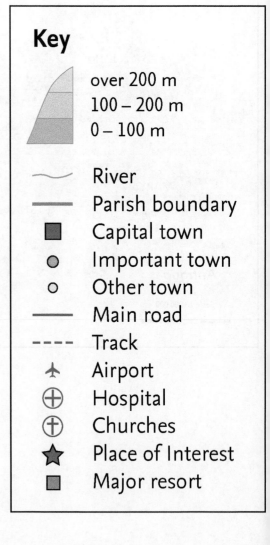

Key

over 200 m
100 – 200 m
0 – 100 m

~ River
— Parish boundary
◼ Capital town
● Important town
○ Other town
— Main road
---- Track
✈ Airport
⊕ Hospital
✝ Churches
★ Place of Interest
◼ Major resort

4 How does a community work?

We are learning to:

- understand physical and social needs
- understand how needs and wants are different
- name the jobs done by people in the community, the places where they work and the tools they use
- understand how people in another part of the world live
- say how communities around the world meet their needs
- name physical features in the community
- understand what happens when people don't work.

What do people need?

People have physical needs and social needs in order to live the best life they can.

Physical needs

These are the basic things that people need to survive. They include ...

... food to eat

... water to drink

... a place to live

37

... clothes to wear   *... and air to breathe.*

Social needs

Human beings are social. This means that, in order to be happy, they need to have other people around them and to feel that they belong to each other. In families, parents do this for children. As you grow up, you have more friends, then probably a partner to love and who will love you.

The people who live in a community also need to help and support each other.

The difference between needs and wants

Needs are things that we must have in order to survive. For example, a plant needs water. Without it, it will die. It is the same for humans. We need water, food, shelter and air to keep us alive and well.

Wants are the things that are not necessary for us to survive but that we may like to have because they make our life easier or more fun. Examples of wants include cars, cellular phones, toys, video games, computers, microwaves and washing machines.

Working for each other in the community

Adults work to earn the money to provide for the basic needs (and some of the wants!) of themselves and their family. Some workers produce goods, while others provide a service. Goods are items that we can buy and sell. People who provide a service do not have anything to sell but work to provide a service to other people.

Sometimes, the work a person does takes them away from their home community to work somewhere else. For example, farmers in the countryside grow their crops and then go into town to sell them to the people there.

Here are some of the people in our community who work to provide us with things we need:

Police officers

The police keep us safe by protecting us from criminals. They are based at a police station. There are several police stations in Antigua. The main one is at American Road in St. John's.

Police officers use two-way radios, guns and handcuffs to help them in their work. They use cars, jeeps and motorcycles to travel from one place to the next. Most of them wear a uniform.

Teachers

Teachers help children learn the things they need to know. They work in schools and use tools such as books, computers, radio, television, the internet and projectors to help them.

Farmers

Farmers use the land to grow crops such as fruits and vegetables and to rear animals. They sell what they produce to feed the people in the community. The farmers grows crops such as tomatoes, potatoes, cucumbers and sweet potatoes. From the animals we get milk, meat, cheese and eggs. The tools the farmers use include tractors, milking machines, crop sprayers and forks.

Fishers

Fishermen and women go to sea to catch a variety of sea creatures. These include lobsters, conchs, fish, shrimps and turtles. These are sold as food back on the land. They use a boat and a net in order to do their work.

Doctors and nurses

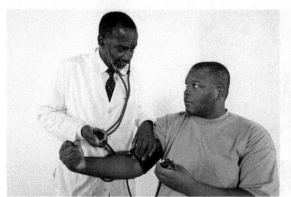

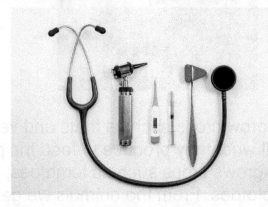

Doctors and nurses work to keep us healthy and to help us to get well when we are sick. They work at the clinics and health centres around Antigua and Barbuda, as well as at the hospital. They use tools like a stethoscope, thermometer and syringe.

Sanitary workers

Sanitary workers collect the garbage and other waste products that we create. They use a garbage truck to do the collection, which they then take to the waste disposal centre. They use gloves to protect their hands.

Bakers

Bakers bake the bread that we eat. Bread is a very important food for many people in the community. Bakers use an oven in the bakery shop to bake the bread.

Postmen/women

Postmen and women provide a service by delivering mail to the people in the community. They are based at a post office. They usually walk from door-to-door but recently some have started driving.

Tailors and seamstresses

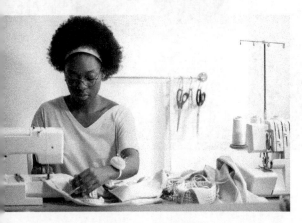
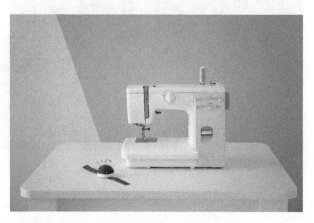

Tailors and seamstresses provide a service by making and altering clothes for us. Most work from home. Some of the tools they use include a sewing machine, thread, needles and scissors.

Carpenters

Carpenters use wood to make houses and furniture for people in the community. They use tools like a saw, hammer and nails.

Firefighters

Firefighters work to keep us safe by putting out fires. When there is a fire, they come very quickly in their fire trucks. They are based at the fire station and wear a uniform. They use tools like a hose, a mask and water boots.

Communities around the world

Some countries in other parts of the world are similar to Antigua and Barbuda. Others are very different. Some countries are smaller, while others are much bigger. The United States of America, for example, is a very large country. Although Antigua and America are not far away from each other, the two countries are very different.

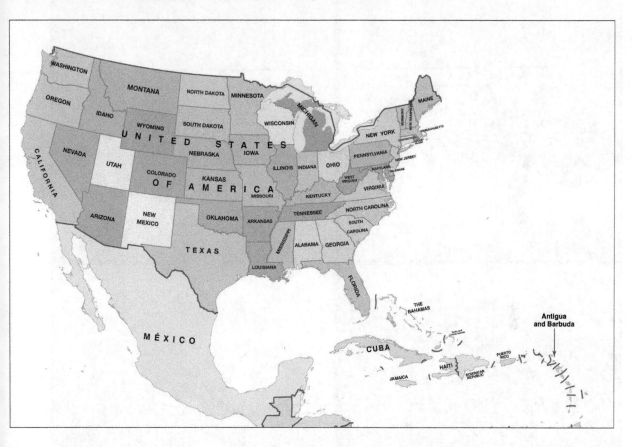

This section looks at what life is like for people in America.

Weather

In America, especially in the north, there are four very different seasons in the year: spring, summer, autumn and winter. This picture gives you an idea of what each season is like.

People need to wear different clothes in different seasons. In spring and summer they wear light clothes but in winter they have to wear very warm clothes, with gloves and boots, so that they don't get cold.

Homes and transport

A lot of people live in apartments, in very tall blocks. The homes are heated in winter and use air-conditioning to keep cool in summer.

Most people have their own car but trains and buses are also used. Because the country is so big, people often fly from one city to another.

Food and sport

Americans grow a lot of crops on a large scale because they have so much land. Huge farms grow wheat to make flour. There are lots of fruit trees, especially oranges and apples. Some farmers rear animals such as cows and chickens.

The most popular sports are football and baseball. Basketball and ice hockey are also very popular, especially in the winter.

The USA has a lot of fast-food restaurants, where people can get a quick meal.

How people around the world meet their needs

Around the world, everyone has the same needs – food, water, a home and clothes. How they meet their needs varies from one country to another. Just as in the USA, the weather makes a lot of difference. It affects the food, the clothes, and often the type of homes people live in.

Some countries have a lot more industry, too, and different sorts of transport.

Physical features of Antigua and Barbuda

There are a number of physical features that make up the landscape of Antigua and Barbuda. Some of these are **natural** features, and some of them are **man-made**.

The natural features include hills, swamps, caves, beaches, lagoons, reservoirs and rainforests.

Mount Obama is the highest point in Antigua and Barbuda.

Antigua is famous for its beautiful beaches. This is Turners Beach.

The man-made features are anything made by humans and include buildings (such as houses, churches, hotels), roads and bridges.

V.C. Bird International Airport is probably our largest man-made physical feature.

When people can't work

Adults work to earn money to provide their basic needs. Sometimes that is not possible. If a person is unable to work, we say they are **unemployed**. There are different reasons why this can happen:

- There are no jobs available.
- The place where they used to work has closed.
- They are ill or disabled.

If a person is unemployed, that can bring problems. They may become depressed. If the family depends on them to bring in money, the whole family may not have enough money for their needs.

The effect of unemployment on Antigua and Barbuda

About 1 in 10 adults is unemployed at any one time. As well as being difficult for the unemployed person, it also affects the country:

- Some families do not have enough money to live on, so need help from the Government.
- They pay less tax to the Government, so the Government has less money.
- There can be a rise in crime as people steal in order to get food.

5 Transportation

We are learning to:

- understand what the word 'transportation' means
- list ways people in the community move around
- name types of transportation and give examples of each
- name transportation centres and their workers
- list transportation rules
- say what the Transportation Board does
- understand how life has changed because of modern transportation.

What is transportation?

Transportation is anything that is used to get people and goods from one place to another. We need to move every day. We move from home to go to school, to work, to church, to the supermarket, and maybe to a restaurant to eat. If it is too far to walk, we need a form of transport to get us to and from those places.

Different ways to travel

People move around the community by walking, or by using bicycles, cars, trucks, vans and buses. Boats are used to transport people between Antigua and Barbuda. Some means of transport are much faster than others.

Land

You can see all the main forms of land transport here. They are all used in Antigua, except for the train.

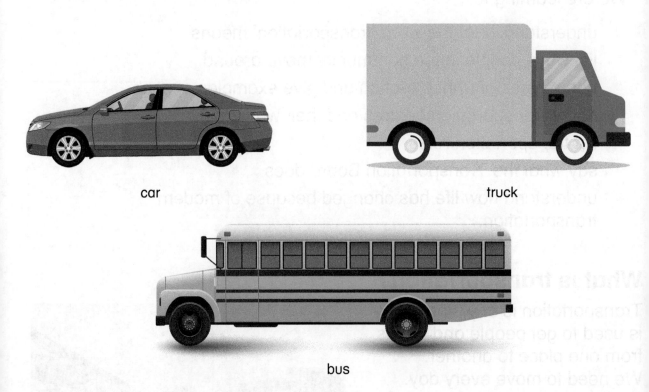

car

truck

bus

Water

This form of transport uses water to get from one place to the next. Usually this is across the sea but rivers can be used inland. Water transport uses ships, boats, ferries and yachts.

Air

Air transport uses airplanes, private jets and helicopters. Air transport is faster than sea transport for moving people and goods from one place to another.

Transportation centres

Transportation centres are the main places we go to when we need to travel somewhere.

Bus stations

The transportation centre for public buses is the bus station. There are two bus stations in Antigua and Barbuda, the West bus station and the East bus station. They carry passengers to different parts of the island. There are bus stops at different places on the way, for passengers to get on

and off. Workers at the bus station include the drivers, conductors and security officers. Passengers pay to get on the bus.

The airport

V.C. Bird International Airport is the only place to take an airplane – for example, if you wanted to leave the island to go to Miami. The airport is located in Coolidge, in the parish of St. George.

The workers at V.C. Bird International Airport include pilots, cabin crew, reservation clerks, ticketing agents, immigration officers and customs officers. Next to the airport is a heliport, for helicopters to take off and land.

Harbours

There are lots of harbours in Antigua and Barbuda, for people who need to take a boat. Heritage Quay is where the cruise ships dock. Small boats dock at English Harbour and Jolly Harbour. St. John's Harbour or Deepwater Harbour is where goods are transported in and out of the country. Workers at the harbour include the ship captains, the crews, dockers, security officers and customs officers.

Jolly Harbour

Many cruise ships dock at Heritage Quay.

Train station

Countries that have a railway sytem have another transportation centre, called a train station. Some large cities have trains that run underground, too.

The London Underground

Keeping safe

Travel can be dangerous, so there are rules that you must follow. This is true when you use the school bus, a public bus, or just walk along the road or sidewalk. When you are on foot, you are called a **pedestrian**.

Here are the main rules for using the bus:

- Sit in your seat at all times.
- Don't put your head or hands out of the window.
- Don't eat or drink inside the bus.
- When you ask the school bus to stop, wait for the conductor to cross you over the road. For a public bus, cross the road in front of the bus and not behind.
- Keep your noise level down so that you don't distract the driver.

And here are the main rules for pedestrians:

1. Always walk on the side of the road, except when crossing the road.
2. Walk facing the traffic coming towards you, so that you can see when a car is coming.
3. Use a pedestrian crossing to cross the road if at all possible.
4. Before you cross the road, look right and then left and then right again, to make sure it is safe.
5. At the traffic lights, wait until the sign says WALK and cars have come to a complete stop, before you cross the road.

Always walk facing the traffic coming towards you.

How the government can help

Every year there are more and more cars on the road. This is especially true in the mornings, when children are going to school and parents are going to work. The roads are more dangerous and traffic jams are becoming a big problem.

Morning rush hour in St. John's

What can the government do to help?

- Build new roads.
- Encourage people to carshare or to use public transport.
- Put in more lighting and illuminated signs.
- Put in speed bumps, especially near schools.

The Transport Board

The Antigua and Barbuda Transportation Board is the Government organisation responsible for our roads. Here are some of the things they do:

1. Issue a driver's licence to someone once they have passed their driving test.
2. Make sure all vehicles are in good driving condition.
3. Put up road signs and paint signs on the street for drivers and pedestrians to follow.

4. Provide buses to take students to and from school.

5. Provide traffic wardens to help the police make sure that traffic rules are obeyed.

The ABTB provides buses to take students to and from school.

How has transport changed our life?

A long time ago there were no cars or buses. Everyone walked. It took a long time to get to where you were going.

Today, walking a long way is a thing of the past. Many people now have their own car and, even if you don't, there are buses and taxis to take you where you want to go quickly. It is much easier and faster to get from one place to another.

At the same time, it has brought some new problems. People don't want to walk and this is damaging their health because they don't do enough exercise. The traffic jams can make everything slower again – and bring more air pollution, which is also bad for health.

So modern transport is a mix of good and bad.

6 Looking after our community

We are learning to:

- understand the words 'pollution' and 'conservation'
- explain how people use natural resources
- say how resources are wasted, and how to conserve them
- describe how to throw out garbage
- understand the weather and how it affects natural resources.

Protecting our local community

Resources are the things you have to help you survive and do well. Man-made resources are things like clothes, a building, and a table. **Natural resources,** shown here, are the things we find in the environment around us, like sunlight, air, trees, water, people, animals and soil.

Trees and plants

Trees and plants are some of the great natural resources of Antigua and Barbuda. We have a wide variety of them in our community. They include: mango trees, guava trees, lime, lemon, orange and grapefruit trees, sugar apple trees, coconut trees, paracetamol bush, mint bush, fever grass or lemongrass, cherry tree, plum guinep, raspberry, domes, and seaside grapes.

Guava   Lemongrass   Guinep

Seaside grapes   Mint

We use this natural resource for food, like fruits and vegetables. The leaves from some plants are used to make tea and medicines. Trees also give us wood, which we can use to make furniture and as materials for buildings. Trees provide food and a home for many animals, birds and insects. Some plants help to purify the air in our homes.

Animals

Some animals are used for meat. Some animals, like donkeys and horses, are used for transportation. Some animals are also used for pets.

Pigs provide us with pork and bacon.

Dogs are very popular as pets.

Land

Humans cannot live in the sea, so we must have land. We need land to build our homes, schools and all our other buildings. Where the soil is good, we use land to grow all the crops that we eat, and to feed our animals.

Water

Water is used for many things, including to drink, to cook food and to wash so that we stay clean and healthy. Without water, we cannot live, and nor can the plants and trees.

The sea is home to fish and other sea creatures. Seawater also provides many homes with drinking water, once it has been treated by the water generating plants.

We must drink water to live and stay healthy.

Wasting our resources

Natural resources can run out. It is easy to waste our resources by being careless.

- When you leave the faucet running, it wastes water.
- If we cut down trees without replacing them, we have fewer trees.
- Taking eggs from animals reduces the number of that type of animal. For example, turtles like to lay their eggs on the sand, and some people like to take the eggs.

How to conserve our resources

In order to make sure that our natural resources do not run out we need to **conserve** them. This means we have to use them wisely. To conserve our resources we can use these three Rs:

REDUCE REUSE RECYCLE

Here are some ideas:

- Reduce the amount of water we waste by reusing it to water the plants.
- Turn off the faucet when you are not using it.
- Limit the length of time you use the shower.
- Don't leave the water running when you are washing your hands.
- Reuse paper and plastic bags and recycle plastic bottles to make other things that can be used around the home.

- Plant new trees to replace ones that are cut down.
- Observe all the conservation rules, for example, no catching of lobster during the off-season.

Learn from the past

The Amerindians, who first came to Antigua, were very good at conserving natural resources. If they wasted them, they would soon have run out, and then they would have nothing. They couldn't buy things they didn't have.

They used the land for growing crops and rearing the animals. They used the water from the river to water the plants and also for transportation. They used every part of the animal, including using the bones to make their tools. They took good care of the land because it helped them to survive.

Pollution

It is very important to keep our land and our community clean. One way of keeping it clean is by disposing of garbage correctly. We should not litter, that is throw away garbage on the ground. Littering can contaminate drinking water and make us sick. Always throw your garbage into a bin that is well covered.

Weather

The weather is things like rain, sunshine and wind. It's what the air feels like and how warm it is. It can change very quickly, so it might be sunny this morning and rainy this afternoon. Sometimes the weather can be dramatic.

In the Caribbean, we are used to lots of hot, sunny weather.

Very strong winds can cause a lot of damage.

The rain can be very heavy, particularly at some times of the year.

Clouds can be very beautiful.

We don't have snow, but some places in the world have a lot of snow.

The weather affects our lives – what we do, such as going to the beach, and what we wear. For some people, like farmers, the weather is very important.

How the weather affects natural resources

The weather can affect our natural resources. For example, heavy rain can cause soil erosion, when the top layer of soil is washed away. That makes it very difficult for farmers to grow their crops.

When there is no rain, plants don't get the water they need to grow. If the plants die, animals have nothing to eat and they may die, too. There may not be enough for us humans to eat.

Hurricanes can destroy many plants and trees, too.

7 Communicating

We are learning to:

- understand the word 'communication'
- say why communication is important
- list communication centres and their workers
- say how people communicated years ago, compared with today
- say how social media is used to communicate.

What is communication?

When we give a message to someone else, we are **communicating**. We might say it, we might write it, and we might show it, for example by giving someone a hug.

Communication is very important. It lets us say what we feel, it lets us learn things, and we need to do it in everyday life, for example to say how much you liked some food or to ask if you can borrow a pencil at school.

What do we need to communicate?

To communicate, we need:

1. A **sender** – the person who is sending the message

2. A **channel** – what you are using to send the message

3. A **receiver** – the person who receives the message

Types of communication

Communication can be **verbal** and **non-verbal**. Verbal communication means using words, either face to face or using a phone, for example. Writing is verbal communication, too. Non-verbal communication doesn't use words. If you smile or frown, you are using non-verbal communication. Other examples include pictures and signals.

Can you work out what this man is communicating in each photo?

Communication in the past

Today, we are used to being able to communicate very quickly with someone, even if they are far away. Long ago, communication was very slow. People used drums, bells, horns, birds and even smoke from a fire to send messages. For verbal communication, they might have to walk long distances in order to pass on a message.

Communication today

Today, there are lots of ways to communicate. These include:

- Telephone
- Radio and television
- Newspaper
- Loudspeaker
- Fax
- Email
- Letter
- Sign language
- Social media

Communication these days is much faster, especially now we have the internet. We can communicate easily with people far away and with lots of people at the same time. The message is received and the response is given almost instantly. We often use email instead of writing letters. And with mobile phones, we can communicate when we're out and about, instead of having to stay put if you are using a landline.

Communication centres

Communication centres are places responsible for sending and receiving messages. There are several in Antigua and Barbuda.

The post office

When you want to send a letter to someone, within Antigua and Barbuda or overseas, you go to the post office. You buy a stamp, place it on your letter and the workers take

it away. It is then taken by mail van, or maybe plane, to its destination. When the person replies to your letter, it comes back through the post office and is delivered to you by the postman.

The workers in the post office sell stamps, sort the mail according to its destination and deliver all the mail received to people in the country.

Control tower

This is the control tower at V.C. Bird International Airport. This is a special sort of communication centre used to communicate with pilots so that they can land a plane safely. The workers at the control tower also make sure planes in the air keep a safe distance from each other.

Telecom centres

Digicel centre in Antigua

Telecom centres are the centres used by mobile phone companies and landline phones. Telecom centres in Antigua include APUA INET, FLOW, and Digicel.

Media houses

Radios, televisions and newspapers also allow people to send and receive messages. People listen to the radio, watch television and read newspapers for information, and for entertainment. The workers in these centres collect information and broadcast it to people in the country. This might be news items, weather forecasts and community notices. ABS television station is a media house in Antigua and Barbuda.

Getting the message across

When you are communicating with someone, it is important to be polite and to get your message across clearly. Here are some ways to do this:

- Look someone in the eye when you are speaking to them.
- Listen when someone is talking to you and don't interrupt.
- Be polite, saying 'please' and 'thank you', for example.
- Speak clearly.
- Be friendly when you answer the phone.
- Be sure the person has finished speaking before you hang up the phone.
- Write the address of the person you are sending the letter to clearly, to make sure that they receive it.
- Keep email messages short and to the point.

Social media

More and more people today use social media to communicate. Especially popular are Facebook, Twitter, WhatsApp, Facebook Messenger, Instagram, TikTok and Snapchat. This is often done using a mobile phone, but can be on a laptop or tablet. The most popular social media app with young people at the moment is Instagram, which lets you easily share photos, videos and messages. It may not be long before it is replaced by a new form of social media, however!

Instagram and TikTok are two popular social media platforms.